CAN THE DANDELIONS BE TRUSTED?

Katherine Gallagher

Can The Dandelions Be Trusted?

2024

Published by Arc Publications,
Nanholme Mill, Shaw Wood Road
Todmorden OL14 6DA, UK
www.arcpublications.co.uk

978 1911469 56 8 (pbk)

Design by ony Ward
Printed in Great Britain by
TJ Books, Padstow, Cornwall

Cover image: © Pierre Vella

Arc Publications UK and Ireland Series:
Series Editor: Tony Ward

A tree grew inside my head.
A tree grew in.
Its roots are veins,
its branches nerves,
thoughts its tangled foliage…

There, within. inside my head,
the tree speaks.

OCTAVIO PAZ

CONTENTS

PART 4

PART ONE

CAN THE DANDELIONS BE TRUSTED?

My garden knows me but that doesn't stop it
being tricky – marigolds pouting as if they've just discovered
their proper name *calendulas*, wanting to make a step up,
cosmos moving centre-stage, leaning this way and that,
perhaps trying to avoid slugs who seem equally partial to pansies.
The dandelions are springing up everywhere, reminding me
of their tendency to crowd it all. Irises, lost in the confusion,
keep sprouting strong leaves, ignoring commands to produce flowers
to balance the valerian's staid blooms. These in turn
are crowding out anemones who make the case for being
genuine survivors
while the roses march on, complaining about my pruning indeed,
nodding to the honeysuckles and lavenders, all of them overshadowed
by the ungainly ash tree, never backward in imposing itself.

DELPHI SONNET

Butterflies weave in and out in a chorus-line,
Clouded Yellows, Red Admirals, Meadow Browns,
kaleidoscopic among wildflowers – dandelions, daisies,
buttercups – yellows, mauves, whites.
This is Apollo's dell, a patchwork of colours and light.
The butterflies have travelled miles here to the southern slopes
of Mount Parnassus, with its scattered tombs and ruins –
a sacred place, almost returned to itself,
grasses carpeting silences. Nearby is a temple of love.
I think of those who have walked these paths,
and of history's many lovers, long buried now.
Where would we be without love? A question
we might ask the Oracle. The sun beats heavy
from an azure sky – I shall carry it with me.

'THE TIDES ARE IN OUR VEINS'

Robinson Jeffers

I St Kilda, Melbourne

Childhood's first trip to the sea,
discovering, slicing waves –
aware deep-down of water's menace
but also its embrace, surfacing and holding
within the pull of blue – restless,
this song of cobalt. Here the unspent ocean,
a walk for shells marking the shore,
rock crabs, resilient.

II On the Lido, Venice

White rocks lined by a wash of sapphire,
the fringed splash against stone.
Turquoise held under forests of cloud,
with sky clearing as water shimmers
through late-evening sun,
its long bars, gold laid across waves,
gentling as boats head back to the islands,
and dusk shades in.

III Beachfront, Margate

Salt on our bodies side by side –
the afternoon's moods, its beckoning waves
cerulean, wraparound, with tides that shepherd us
in a dance of water, curtained spray,
mazarine rinsed to perfection,
homing into shore
a landscape of hearts that stay intact
keeping steady, secrets of the sea.

iv Trapani, Sicily

Easy the trails of movement
in tune with sea's promise of forever,
a spell of ultramarine
that plays in the mind's eye,
an aqua-filled islet shoring minute pebbles –
each, individual in its way as the giant rocks
mapping the coast, and the long horizon's
zipped meeting with sky.

EARLY MORNING, LAKE MONTE GENEROSO

No one is swimming in the clear lake. All is still
except where a fisherman throws in his line.
He winds back the reel again, again.
A fish leaps behind him as if it were a game.
And now the day scoops out its usual place
as sun's first shifts slip over the mountain,
flushed, clearing, fresh.

I'm in love with the lake and this calm
that I cannot pocket, take with me,
as engines rev up, the first campers leave,
and a steam-train pulls around the lake's rim.
Smoke-coils lift over the road
that runs alongside houses – burnished, mirrored
on the water's fine skin.

BROOMFIELD PARK

A moorhen busies herself,
rocks this way and that
on a wave-washed nest.

Swans float in late-afternoon chill,
shadows lengthen,
chestnut buds swell.

Forsythia stirs the breeze –
pastel-green willows barely move,
dipping branch-tips into the lake.

Every year I wait for this –
first flowers, trees leafing
on sculpted branches,

reflecting in the water
their trembling
cascades of green.

TREE-WATCH AND GREEN CINQUAINS

'The poetry of earth is never dead.'
JOHN KEATS

Leaders
of Planet Earth
gather in a health-spa,
float the feeling of *bonhomie*
up close.

Fight for
ancient forests,
our chance, a mended life.
Under Euston Square, earth-lovers
protest.

Robins
lighten the dusk,
pure notes quivering, sharp
rivulets of neighbourliness –
marked time.

Tree-watch
remembering
when you first hugged a tree.
That was a kind of beginning,
heart-sure.

COUNTING THE SWANS

Inspired by W.B. Yeats's 'The Wild Swans at Coole'

We're approaching Coole Park, thinking of the swans and Yeats's poem. It's October again and we half expect the great poet himself to come stalking down these lanes. The trees are in their autumn beauty, the woodland paths are dry. His words echo. It's his nineteenth year of seeing the swans on the lake.

> *the desire to linger –*
> *the wanderer in you asks*
> *what's more beautiful than this*

Suddenly we see the birds, afloat, not the fifty-nine seen by Yeats. Today, twenty. We count them again, excited, unbelieving that we've seen them – claimants of these waters. They take their time, gliding at ease. The air wraps itself around.

> *the spell of Ireland and Yeats*
> *fills us with history*
> *the mystery of swans*

We have come so far, wanting to see them. They seem content to stay forever under this mid-autumn sky. No, suddenly they lift their heads, take off

> *necks outstretched*
> *steady wingbeats*
> *my memory of Coole*

OWNING THE WAVE

She shares the wave
holds it, knows the song
they weave through,
the lick of salt on their tongues,
scherzos of moments edging waves
that curl over and over,
a rondo of sharing.

Call it love, this desire to hold,
sealing days in a glide of hours
the tremendous wave waiting
within a miraculous sweep.

LES LUMIÈRES DE PARIS

From way off out of darkness, we saw it,
city glittering, streets garlanded,
radiating out in frosty air – Place de la Concorde,
Madeleine, Notre Dame, Tour Eiffel, Quartier Latin,
Abbesses. the climb up to Montmartre where
Van Gogh had toiled under these lights,
breath of the Seine edging the city's heartbeat,
famous bridges haloed, encapsulating journeys,

tourists clasping history, with Sacré Coeur's nineteenth century-
basilica overlooking all. The flower-stall holders
calling for customers. Crowded cafes, restaurants,
bars, pâtisseries, open to sell their wares,
everything illumined by fierce evening light
rivalling daytime, and a meal out to celebrate *Les Fêtes*,
an invitation to savour food for soul and eye –
the whole city dining in one awaited spectacle,

friends, parents, children, scarved, mittened,
the party partying on, and Père Noel
sky-jingling, turning the day on its head –
atmosphere framed by *bonhomie* and markets,
chance meetings, so many drawn to the celebrations,
this gaiety of blending – reclaiming colours
under lights, as though nothing could go unnoticed

in this walk-walk city. We had seen the world hush
for the shortest day, skies darkening over.
And now the solstice gloom had turned to light,
holding us, real as our venturing, shaped by
days drawing in, beckoning us towards
blazes of colour, neon illuminations
that would stay with us for the year to come.

WISHES

for B

I wish it was summer and that I was somewhere hot.
I wish I could bake cream puffs like my mother.
I wish I could see my parents again, even briefly.
I wish I could swim with dolphins.
I wish for the pure songs of robins.
I wish for the clarity of afternoons.
I wish for silver linings.
I wish I was travelling with you –
to new places, taking our time.

PART TWO

THE USES OF SNOW

2 a.m. in a taxi. Suddenly the city's
a flaring continent – white,
delivering sights from an exotic film set,
Westminster, Big Ben, the Victoria Memorial –
she's some character in her element,
flakes shawl together,

heavier by the minute.
To the right, Hyde Park's iced fields –
hinterlands invaded, white ruling the night
putting its face on a different Christmas,
returning home to North London, she reminds herself,
as flurries clog the windscreen…

So little happens just by accident,
her change of countries, an aloneness
she's grown into, away not a year yet,
finding new spaces. This is 1969 –
there'll be many more years away,
a hemisphere's width of markers.

Choose your year, find a life –
never in ages will it be against
a backdrop of such eerie whiteness as this –
London remade, blanched over,
proclaiming softly
how to start again.

EARLY DAYS IN PARIS

You know about the legends –
Joyce and Eliot, Hemingway's
'movable feast', the writer-gatherings
at La Closerie des Lilas,
and you visit Shakespeare's
English bookstore opposite Notre Dame –
browse, write a few notes, buy postcards.

You sense the exhilaration, Place St Michel
with its memories of '68, there
stretching before you, with streets of cafés
and the savoury edge of Rue Mouffetard,
lingering, rich, among billboards of films,
the aura of French couture,
sculptures and galleries everywhere you turn.
You are swept into this newness, iconic bridges,
Concorde, La Tour Eiffel, the Tuileries,
Rue de Rivoli, Jeu du Paume –

you walk and walk, amazed and heady,
stop at the Louvre, knowing Paris is a place
where you want to be curious,
speak French, get to the heart of it,
imbibe its atmosphere of poets and writers,
artists who walked the Seine, its environs,
people who love the food, music, films and art
in a city that built itself through centuries,
that never took itself for granted.

PARIS ROND-POINT

creamy buildings
                catch the last
                sunset-
                        pink

leaves drift
                tangled against
                railings
                        fluttering

people stream past
                hurrying
                clutching their evening-
                        papers

lovers hand in hand
                stop and kiss
                pick up a golden leaf
                        share it

RETROSPECT

She crawls across India, bus-slow –
weeks alone have made her anxious,
looking forward, looking back.
She hunts wide blanks of sky,
sees him everywhere, the weight of it
burning through her days.

In this country's vastness,
villages and people are mindful, steady.
She sees palaces, walks in time
with painted elephants, watches people bathe
in the Ganges, pray, burn their dead.
Jaipur, Agra, Benares, cities wake her whole.

At each hotel, the smell of laurel
lifts a clear cerulean sky.
The soft night air slides over
a day of cameos, heavy-shouldered vultures
picking bones, cloudless skies,
people who love their gods,
Brahma, Vishnu, Shiva – the spirit
of this place. Slowly she is learning to accept
his absence, an ocean away now –
this being alone, being herself.

TIGER

This is the grass that lured the tiger
that walked by rivers as of right.

This is the song which led the tiger
that danced unreined before the fight.

This is the sky that knew the tiger,
that flamed its heart in rings of light.

This is the dream which raised the tiger,
that traced its lair and shored its might.

This is the space that called the tiger,
which fed it, led it, steadying, bright.

This is the field that blessed the tiger
as each day's sun burned into night.

DON'T CRY FOR

old love-affairs
wedged in history, fixed

like faces on a film
pinning you to that younger self,

times when your heart told you
this was not a death

though it felt like it,
as if part of you were sinking.

Still, the survivor in you said
there was no other way but forward

as you toyed with chances
of escaping back into yourself.

You didn't want to think of endings.
This was a love you'd set years on.

What would you say to him today –
taking leave, sun on his back?

SONG FOR MY DONEGAL ANCESTORS

1

Did you start out as farmers
in love with the peat and the trees?

Were you clever makers and carpenters
intent on tracing a way?

How many of you were fishermen
ready to take on the sea?

What was it made you happy?
Did you like to stand up and sing?

Were you bone-crazy for football,
and racing around a pitch?

Or horsemen, keeping some stables
to glean your slow time away?

I wonder what you looked like?
Did you have ocean-deep eyes

and wild dreams to lure you
towards some imagined new start?

Did you have money and lose it,
living with the pain and the shame?

Did you have long lives or early deaths
secure in the fear of God –

with big families, clan-close or divided,
wanting a bit more from life?

How many sang Faith of our Fathers
on a living treadmill of prayer?

And my mothers – colleens or witches?
Were you pursuing your lives

under wraps and plans, quietly,
alongside the men and the boys?

Did you start out as mothers' helpers
governessing for local grandees?

Did you spend your days doing housework,
making cakes, maybe dresses for a ball?

2

Did you decide to walk out one day,
say you just weren't coming back?

Were you smart Catholic girls, hen-sure,
in a hurry to find the right man?

Or were you tempted to accept God's call
to be the chosen one, nun of the family?

Were you performers, playing the piano,
and singing with special charm?

Did you ride horses like your brothers.
and star in gymkhanas nearby?

How many of you were bookish and shy,
keeping ideas close-knit like prayer,

with all the zest and passion of the Irish,
wild mountains and rain in your souls?

This poem, originally published in a shorter form as 'Poem for
my Ancestors' in *Poetry Salzburg Review*, No. 3, 2017, has been
added to, in order to 'elaborate' on the lives of my 'mothers' as
well. Actually, as in the following poem 'Paths' (p.32), my great
grandfather left from Derry in 1857 / 58 for Australia, where the
gold rush was in full swing in Victoria in the area around Mal-
don. He apparently jumped ship at Melbourne, went to Maldon
and never returned.

PATHS

I went
to the old town
of Derry to take in
the tall ships of my forefathers –
clippers.

There was
the walled city –
I imagined life then,
my great grandfather leaving with
nothing.

A young
ship's carpenter
on his way overseas,
taking the route to Australia
in hope,

after
the Great Famine,
eighteen fifty-seven,
the dead walking streets, Donegal-
spectres.

In the
new museum,
I was told he'd have walked
barefoot, shoes in hand, to the boat,
young lad

later
disembarking,
heading north to Maldon
and stories of gold to be found,
with luck.

IN THE FAITH

i.m. Mary Phelan

My grandmother couldn't
sing in tune. Music-lover,
she walked tall, wanting
everyone to join in.

So the family sang from habit
the way birds might – popular songs,
Memories, The Sunshine
of Your Smile.

We learnt the importance
of being ready to sing at will.
In my ten-year-old maze,
I imagined that was how the saints

and martyrs managed, even
if walking on hot coals.
When we trumpeted Faith of Our Fathers,
the words entered our hearts, gusting belief,

How it held us together, despite
ourselves, in spite of everything outside –
illnesses, deaths, droughts
that threatened, kept edging in.

MARGARET, DANCING

When Margaret penned her proposal
to Eastville's most eligible bachelor –
farmer Tommy Robb, Esq – the district knew
the season had started fortuitously.

Margaret brought flowers and light
to his dry patch of terrain,
marked out the farm into airy spaces, weaving
around clumps of ringbarked trees,

and she and Tom, virginal, fiftyish, danced
like young things, throwing off their years
in moon-spurred reels and bagpipe-skirls
as piper Alex, kilted and medallioned,

brought The Banks of Loch Lomond
to the lowlands of Eastville, giving the nod
to promises and lift-off for all who loved
and danced, danced and loved.

A PASSIONATE HEART

'I want to be more than my verses – I want to be this person who once lived here'.

MARY GILMORE (1864-1962)

In Dobell's portrait, she is ninety-one, serene,
silver-haired, lace at her neck.
She plays it regally in voluminous black –

a doyenne, about to give the speech of her life,
wistful eyes glinting over a set mouth – her gloved hands
belie her spread of work still to be done.

She has the solidity of sculpture – Dame Mary Gilmore,
legend-making, seeing her city change,
as it has changed her.

She holds the arms of her chair as if to steady herself,
staring ahead, protective of her nine decades,
politics, poetry.

Words burn in her palm. Though
dressed like a queen, she has known
a life of scrubbing floors, scrubbing words . . .

Her life was words – words shone as a torch lighting up.
Paraguay, back to Australia. From one different world
to another – her search for justice, to renew.

Dame Mary Gilmore, b.orn in Goulbourn, N.S.W., was a writer, poet and activist. After an itinerant childhood, she went to Sydney, trained as a teacher but later turned to writing and journalism. In 1895, she joined William Lane's socialist project in Paraguay, married, but after some time returned to Australia. William Dobell's distinguished portrait of Dame Mary Gilmore hangs in Sydney in the Art Gallery of New South Wales..

ELEGY

i.m. Kevin

1

I am moving towards change,
arriving yet again, recognizing my younger self
in childhood landmarks, haunts.

This time my brother doesn't meet me
at the airport – he has a new
language now, has travelled great

distances, solo. Presently there is a light
through the tunnel that divides us.
Nothing is as new, as real, as this. I try to picture

the scene as if he were my twin and I,
recording our story. I know no camera
could capture this tendrilled light.

2

Now you are flying like a shadow
near my plane, restless,
still in the blue sum of it all –

blue sky meeting blue sea.
The journey sweeps me on,
whirrs into its turquoise.

You'd so wanted to travel,
see green Ireland,
the place you owned in your soul.

You thought you'd find
part of yourself,
something close, a touchstone.

PART THREE

SONG FOR A CITY

Give me a city, glowing
  with buildings, busy
  and fruitful as a field
  ready for farming.

Give me a city calm within,
  that feeds the hungry,
  that will shore up
  the power of hands.

Give me a city of colours,
  tree-mottled, kaleidoscopic
  from yellow fires to rosy dens,
  arcane and blessed.

Give me a city at ease
  with itself, that wears its heart
  boldly, that heralds its river
  with honour and caring.

Give me a city, open
  to the skirr of gatherings,
  channelling one generation
  to the next.

Give me a city, enduring
  and wise, celebrated
  across centuries –
  a cunabula of light.

LINES FOR A GARDEN

I looked out at the steady rain
which was encouraging me to plan, keep trying.
I knew I could get started on the digging,
with no obstacles to a bed of cosmos and daisies.

Indeed, everything inspiring me to keep trying
for this mini-paradise in my mind's eye –
sunny beds of dianthus, cosmos and daisies
and borders of salvia, poppies and sage.

Seeing this mini-paradise in my mind's eye
gradually taking on its own shape,
I was happy with borders of salvia, poppies and sage
backed by rosemary and lavender to bring the bees.

It was slowly taking on its own shape
with a corner patch of greens and scented herbs
backed by rosemary and lavender to bring the bees.
There were few limits now with sweet peas and June lilies,

and a corner patch of greens and scented herbs
alongside trailing roses curled over an arch.
There'd be few limits now with sweet peas and June lilies
and borders edged with irises and gladioli.

THE PIANIST

To think she'd once played for Rubinstein,
fingers lighting The Preludes, freeing her gift –
that future she'd blocked. She'd been foolish,
now had to live with it. She sees it all –
gloves masking her hands,
chafed geographies – the lined palms,
her cuticles' frayed reminders.

He had praised her, a country student,
twenty, travelling to Melbourne for lessons,
a hoped-for break. He'd urged her to study –
London, Paris – the chance of a lifetime.
Her teacher wanted her to take that chance.
She should have dared, could never forgive
her mother's doubts, or worse, her own.

This is a true story from the author's early days.

HER LIFE

She's the kind of woman you sometimes meet
in a shopping mall, head forward, shoulders slumped,
thinking of the money she doesn't have,

sloping towards the exit
where buses and taxis gather.
She's fifty now,

wondering which direction to take,
as though she's wrapped the bones of her life
into a parcel almost too heavy to carry.

MOONWISE

Dear Jane,

Don't think I'm insane,
there's no point in changing your nose.
Sure, you can change it, but who knows,
what if the op. fails? It'll break
your heart, be more than your nerves can take.

Listen, a nose is an outcrop like your toes,
it meets the world head-on – friends and foes,
and changing it, all that pain
could traumatise your brain.
Think of the mess when they have to smash
your face – you'll look like a crash-
victim and you'll just want to be alone,
spend all your time on the phone…

Jane dear, who likes to feel
their beauty go. But it's not such a big deal.
Look, I had my face redone,
botox, chin-tucks,
wrinkles and jowls,
eyelashes, implants – it was life on the run.

A born-again beauty queen,
I got around, was seen
at parties and shows. Great for a while,
I did it in style.

But *tempus fugit.* Now, who'd ever know?

Your old friend,

Misty Glo

47

AMARYLLIS

Amaryllis is solitary, guarded –
named after a shepherdess
who shed her blood to prove true love.

In any sphere she is noticed.
She holds the secret of glamour –
elegant, stately, gracing the wild earth.

She will remind you of her flame
like a lantern in a cave,
or a lighthouse edging dark seas.

SUMMER IN RAILWAY FIELDS

for David Bevan

Close in, there's lavender and a mini-forest of birch,
yew, cherry and ash. Trees planted or self-sown – most magical,
the marriage tree, a cherry and ash entwined.

At the chalet door, a briar-rose, self-seeded
is layered with flowers, surrounded by patches of comfrey,
catmint, cosmos and lemon queen.

Then the speckled woods – brimstone butterflies do their flypast
while a red admiral sweeps before the pond. Bees glide by,
at the back, reeds and yellowflag irises shade the newts.

Alongside, fragrant meadowsweet carries foaming clusters
of creamy flowers, and we're not too late for goatsbeard –
'Jack-go-to-bed-at-noon' – on this sun-filled July day.

Pass by the meadow, stinging nettles, birdsfoot trefoil
housing the caterpillars of the common blue butterfly – nearby,
                                        fodder vetch
with its bright purplish flowers. And everywhere, birdsong –
                                thrush, robin, blue-tit.

Follow the trail past the new meadow with corn marigold,
rosebay willowherb on the left, then the playground and New River,
the convolvulus and wild plums. Pass stinking iris,

the Victorian stench-pipe, the one hundred and fifty-year-old
                                        field maple,
pass the foxes' earth, a few steps up to the old railway tracks
emptied now of coal trucks, back to the chalet via woodland.

The Life of BEIGE

Beige is its own country, captured in a swirl of dust, flaunting sand. Grasshopper-dry on baked lawn. A colour-chart fly-by, indifferent echoes of desert. Beige speaks the language of dry paddocks, roads, tracks, lifted by whirlwinds, gaunt presences whisked about like dry-eyed phantoms, in shades from camel to biscuit, to scorched cream.

Calibrations of RED

Red, the colour that clothed you in its sunset haze, a torch-marker of day's departure. Carry red flowers – cannas, roses, dahlias, flower-stall reds that cheer you, a fire that articulates, the colour the child takes out of the box. Poppy-reds, sunset rain where the horizon lifts endless, for the breakaway pall of bushfires, the fear, announcement. Picture-book reds. The burning celebrations that herald a reckoning from victory to a glimpse of the unknown.

Essences of BLACK

I'm happy with black – mysterious, loaded, invoking magic, the underside of noir, stillness the touch of velvet or flouncy georgette, black, forever invoking fashion, cocktails, Chanel's black dress that looks outward, solo, that goes with everything, that defines otherness, and absence of light. Black, that works the sky's pitch as mystery, steady dark. My companion, to wear with reds, greens, yellows, sharpening the eye. That I don't take for granted, that I wear gladly, my colour to love.

GENEVA SONNET

The Lake boasts its stillnesses –
boats covered, sunset combing clouds
as the *Jet d'Eau* shines satin-white.
Swans draw in and out,
lifting easy, contained as the boats.
Late clouds turn pink, the sky fades
to crystal, a spread of stars.

People pass,
dusky on the Esplanade,
street-lamps glimmer, neons flash –
I feel your presence, calling up memories,
reminders of the choices that we had, how we
threaded them out of our lives,
one by one.

FOR EVA

Living in hiding, 1943-44.

The young girl
in the photograph,
seated at the entrance
to a misty garden, cycled nightly
through Amsterdam's darkened streets
to help the Resistance.

Post-war, she was overtaken
by domestic chores – lost in those
spaces between the cooker,
recipe-books and her daughters.
Everyone praised her modesty,
no-one mentioned her brave past.

At her funeral, her brother declared her
'Fighter in the Dutch Underground',
acknowledging this heroine,
the ethereal girl in the photograph
who'd vanished long ago.

Poem by Nurit Kahana
translated from the Hebrew
by Katherine Gallagher & Nurit Kahana.

LIVING WITH REDBACKS

In my bush schooldays, the redback spider held us in awe – with a bite deadlier than a snake. Our teacher said that only the lady redback was poisonous – likely to be found in dry sheltered places such as lavatories, cubby-houses or letter-boxes. We were warned to be on the lookout.

Then in the girls' outdoor toilet I saw it – under the seat, waiting, small black head, eyes fixed, with big bulbous body marked with a red-jewelled stripe, its strong legs ready to pounce. Trembling and yelling, I ran across the schoolground to my teacher and fellow pupils.

Part of my ten-year-old self is still running.

THE SONG OF THE HAT

for my mother

If there was a Song of the Hat, she perfected it,
the Chanson of Childhood. 'Put on a hat, you'll get sunstroke',
or 'You'll ruin your skin'

Long before the days of ozone-scares,
she was a shade person, smiling under her panama
with a sou'wester close-by, just in case.

STEPS FROM HERSTORY

for C.

1

The surgeon said she was a young seventy-eight.
Sure, her hammertoes were a problem, but…
His soft tones circled her ears.

Could he possibly do something about her toes?
she asked gingerly.
He held her feet, smoothed his hands
over the jutting outcrops, announced he could remove
the offending joints – he'd do both at the same time.
Of course, she'd need lots of rest.

Like a ship finding a new haven she was happy
knowing her rows of matching accessories
would at last be hers for the wearing – shoes,
handbags, green, mushroom, red.

2

carrying a torch
for the language of feet
that cannot be heard
coming closer
the journeys not taken
foot-weary
foot-breaking

A CLEAR LOLLY MOON

a clear lolly moon
keeping counsel
over our road

she sashays slowly
focusing the sky
tide-maker

heavenly-waltzer
serene
in the moment

with no pirouettes
no tango
no cake-walk

she's an old face
at home
in her own skin

PART FOUR

CHARTRES

1

This time, approaching from Orleans,
we didn't see the cathedral looming

against the wheatlands of La Beauce,
but felt its pull, a sacred place

saved to witness and to carry tidings.
We memorise the faces etched in stone – a tryst

with eternity, and more.

2

In the long dusk, light pierces
stained-glass –

Chartres radiating candle-glow
as a singer enters,

asking fabled questions
where each note, each word

is linked to all
that has gone before – the openness

of prayer and beauty gifting travellers,
their pilgrim souls

as finally the cathedral resounds,
spills huge applause.

WHAT I WANT

is to walk in green places, close and spreading,
                                        with trees changing colour –
golds, yellows and reds taking the stage, beeches, oaks
                                        and sycamores
glowing ever brighter in Broomfield Park, alongside
                                        Palmers Green
with its trees, schools and shops, eye-rich, then back home
to Bowes Park, with Myddleton Road's silver birches
                                        and chestnuts
taking their turn at making us light-in-our-skins, rejoicing
among the open-air cafes, shrubs and hanging-baskets
                                        of this busy shopping-street.

And I will take my time and walk the happy nonchalance
of fulsome days, lit with birdsong, the blackbirds out early,
the pocket-park with robins singing full-throated, and
                                        thrushes, nightingales
telling me they are here, that it is a moment for finding
                                        grubs on fruitful stems.
And the New River close-by, home to coots and ducks,
                                        teaching the miracle of water,
the moon rising, and us homing, with a squirrel crossing
                                        our path because it's that time
of the year, maybe even meeting a fox on his midnight prowl.

RAILWAY FIELDS, NORTH LONDON

i.m. June English

We craned our necks
waited
for the swans

So many feathers
on the bank
where they'd nested

This time they had
two cygnets
fluffy-grey

The whole family
serene
a green omen

We hoped they'd
return here again
next year

Claiming the New River
water-lilies
willow-herb

Ash and cherry
grown wilder
with each passing year

VENUS

Why does a clever woman so surprise
especially if she's Venus on a shell
who sees the world through calm unsparing eyes?

The chances are she's tough as well as wise
to all the gaps between heaven and hell.
Why does a clever woman so surprise?

She's Artemis, Persephone – but realise
she's fiery Aphrodite as well,
seeing the world through sharp unstarry eyes.

She may not be the one you'll recognise
until she woos you with a winning spell.
Why does a clever woman so surprise?

See her spurn fawners, boors and fools, prize
her passion, frankness – time will tell.
Why does a clever woman so surprise
who sees the world through sharp unblinkered eyes?

TESTAMENT

This house doesn't complain,
it looks its purpose in the eye with
a northern suburb's hundred-year-old
gift of knowing – in harmony with a sky
which daily declares its season a little closer
to the sun. See it as a space set in clumps of
ruffled garden sizing up the rhythms of winter.
I am not happy in this dark time when sun drags,
holds back I would like some snow-loving Wenceslaus
to reassure me that this sky is not as measured and exacting
as it seems. The mirror-bush, daphne and jasmine sit alongside
the lilac's unleafed branches. I listen for bird-chatter, am grateful
to my unfailing haven, with its solid roof.

THE UNIFORM

Aged eight, mad about aeroplanes and making model-jets
that took on the universe. Cue for his father to send him
to RAAF Officer School. 'You're going. Set you up for life'.

> *Years of limbo. Study and the uniform,*
> *the uniform, don't want to wear it, might die in it,*
> *I'm not your hero.*

Where was he? It wasn't the study that irked.
He'd loved University – a dream-place with real friendships,
best of his life.

> *As for the uniform,*
> *I'm not proud of it, don't want to wear it, might die in it,*
> *I'm not your hero.*

> *Never wanted to join up, to kill anyone,*
> *nor command anyone else to.*

> *And the uniform,*
> *I'm not proud of it, don't want to wear it, might die in it,*
> *I'm not your hero.*

Vietnam, the war was coming closer,
Australia was sending a squadron. He couldn't know
where it would end.

> *As for the uniform*
> *I'm not proud of it, don't want to wear it, might die in it.*

The uniform? Where would it lead him? He couldn't think.
It would lead him to the end of himself.

> *The uniform,*
> *I'm not proud of it, don't want to wear it, might die in it.*
> *I'm not your hero.*

TANKA JOURNEYS

i.m. Edna Shaw

a saxophonist
practises in the alcove –
harmonies rippling,
magpies carolling
in the thick of the bush.

a child tugged along
by hurrying parents
glances enviously
over her shoulder
at rain-filled puddles.

the white magnolia
gleams in the silvery air –
floats catchwords of spring,
the allure of a debutante
a moon floating free from cloud.

my vanishing years
remind me of a young girl
cycling myriad roads,
awed by the impossible
nearness of the stars.

CIRCUIT

Hornchurch Country Park 3rd Age Walk

Eye-sharp, blue flash of a kingfisher, tableau of wagtail, house martin, sky. Mesh the green with the blue of dragonflies, damselflies. Follow the River Ingrebourne to the Thames. Summer – histories under our feet. Turning pages – Stone Age, Bronze Age, Iron Age, Normans, farmers, yeomen of the manors. Their grasslands, marshes, ponds, history in a breath. Heron, frog, fox, rabbit, hedgehog, owl, vole.

Pass by the teasel-gatekeeper, journeying the river, with hemlock, solid purple and poisonous, burdock, shadowed borders of himalayan balsam, interloper, its fresh pink highlighting the bull-rushes, yellow ragwort, oxeye daisies and rosebay willow-herb purpling distances, heron on elderberry.

Walk the heartlands. Talk this geography – white yarrow, gorse, blue chicory, and blazoned poppies, willow, ash, hawthorn, oak. A stretch of park, field upon field, invite ramblers' short-cuts. The story of bird and tree – give and take, take and give. This space once made over to Spitfires – now a park.

Around us, a bird-chorus – woodpecker, chiffchaff, blackbird, willow warbler, skylark, thrush. You're grateful for shade, for each tree, each stand-and-listen spot as Rangers spin the history, old jokes flying. And the meld of it – close by, the river slow-paced, water-level high despite the drought. Peer at fish, try to name them – carp, perch, roach?

Sun makes no concessions, nor do the walkers, eyes seeking clouds – travel at your own pace like the daylight moon lingering shell-soft. Now this floodplain footpath, its valley view on the curve of the Orbital, with a ring of butterflies – meadow browns, tortoise-shells, red admirals, commas, peacocks.

Flat terrain, vast skies opening – the Park wraps itself around us – this Spitfires' airfield still recalling the Battle of Britain, its fighters, part of RAF Hornchurch, their hangars turned into housing estates, their planes long since guided in to landing-strips in the race between strafings.

Everything still now, a home for memories of brave pilots. See Tett Turrets, Pillboxes with photos and explanations. Lightly, it's the slide back, reminders of those times. Some walkers talk burning skies, their childhoods as evacuees. How quickly the grass comes again. Nearby, the spell of water, Ingrebourne Marshes, with mallards, teals, moorhens, lapwings, house martins, skylarks.

Circuit, walk into the habit of walking – under sun under shade by the river, walking, walking memories, walking all your years behind you and ahead.

EPIPHANY

For the bird flying into the sun

For the bird that arrived unnoticed

For the bird that hasn't stopped singing

For the bird that saw bulldozers coming

For the bird flying on through darkness

For the bird that sings in a cage

For the bird that sings in the memory

For those who sing with the bird

BIOGRAPHICAL NOTE

Katherine Gallagher was born in 1935 in Australia, graduating from the University of Melbourne and teaching in Melbourne before moving to Europe in 1969. Living first in London, then in Paris, she moved back to London, where she worked as a secondary school teacher and as a poetry tutor for the Open College of the Arts, Jackson's Lane, Barnet College and Torriano. During this time she co-edited *Poetry London*.

In 1978, she was awarded a New Writer's Fellowship from the Literature Board, Australia Council, and in 1981, she won the Brisbane Warana Poetry Prize. Her book *Passengers to the City* (1985) was shortlisted for the 1986 Adelaide Festival John Bray National Poetry Award and in 1987, she was one of five poets representing Australia at the Struga Poetry Festival.

Her second book, *Fish-rings on Water,* introduced by Peter Porter, appeared in 1989 and in 2000, her third full collection, *Tigers on the Silk Road* was published by Arc. Three further collections followed from Arc: *Circus-Apprentice* (2006), *Carnival Edge* (2010) and *Acres of Light* (2016). Her translation of Jean-Jacques Celly's poetry collection, *Le Somnambule Aux Yeux d'Argile* (The Sleepwalker with Eyes of Clay) was published in 1994

Katherine has received, among other accolades, a Royal Literary Fund Award in 2000 and two London Society of Authors' Foundation Awards, in 2008 and 2021 respectively.

She has read her poetry at festivals and universities in the UK, Australia, Ireland, Germany, Italy and France and her poems have been translated into French, German, Hebrew, Italian, Romanian and Serbo-Croat.

www.katherine-gallagher.com

ACKNOWLEDGEMENTS

'Margaret, dancing' 'In the Faith' and 'Retrospect' appeared in 'Tread Softly… Irish Poets in the U.K.', *Agenda,* Vol 54, Nos. 3 & 4, 2021.

'Broomfield Park' appeared in *Enfield Poets* (Chela Publishing, 2021)

'The Tides are in our Veins' was published in *The New European*, 2018.

'Delphi Sonnet', 'Tiger' and 'Retrospect' appeared in *The South-East Asian Anthology* (Ed. Sudeep Sen, Singapore, 2021).

'Song for my Donegal Ancestors' was published in part as 'Poem for my Ancestors' in the *Poetry Salzburg Review*, No. 3, 2017.

'Paris Rond-Point' was first published in my chapbook *The Eye's Circle* (Rigmarole, Melbourne, 1974)

'Les Lumières de Paris' was published in *Christmas Lights* (Candlestick Press, 2017).

Several tanka were published in the British Haiku Society's Magazine *Blithe Spirit*, 2021.

'A Passionate Heart' was published in the anthology *Of Some Importance* (Grey Hen Press, 2020). 'Early Morning, Lake Monte Generoso' was anthologised in *Measuring the Depth*, (Grey Hen Press, 2020).

Acknowledgments are due to the editors of the following magazines: in the U.K: *Artemis Poetry* (2021), *Brittle Star*, *The Dawn Treader, The French Literary Review*;. in India: *Prosopisia*; and online: *Dust, Allegro Poetry, The High Window* and *London Grip*.